Long Walks in the Afternoon

THE 1982 LAMONT POETRY SELECTION
OF THE ACADEMY OF AMERICAN POETS

From 1954 through 1974 the Lamont Poetry
Selection supported the publication and
distribution of twenty first books of poems.
Since 1975 this distinguished award has been
given for an American poet's second book.

Judges for 1982: June Jordan, Richard Shelton,
and David Wagoner.

Long Walks in the Afternoon

Poems by MARGARET GIBSON

LOUISIANA STATE UNIVERSITY PRESS

BATON ROUGE AND LONDON

1982

This book is for Joanne

Copyright © 1982 by Margaret Gibson
All rights reserved
Manufactured in the United States of America

Designer: Albert Crochet
Typeface: VIP Electra
Typesetter: G & S Typesetters, Inc.
Printer: Thomson-Shore, Inc.
Binder: John Dekker & Sons, Inc.

Grateful acknowledgment is made to the editors of the following
publications, in which some of the poems herein have appeared
previously, sometimes in slightly different form: *Darkhorse,
Embers, Friend's Journal, Hampden Sydney Poetry Review,
Michigan Quarterly Review, Minnesota Review, Nantucket
Review, New Virginia Review, Poet Lore, Poetry, Poets On, Tendril.*

Publication of this book has been supported by a grant from
the National Endowment for the Arts in Washington, D.C., a
federal agency.

LIBRARY OF CONGRESS CATALOGING IN PUBLICATION DATA

Gibson, Margaret.
    Long walks in the afternoon.
    I. Title.
PS3557.I1916L6   811'.54   82-275
ISBN 0-8071-1017-5   AACR2
ISBN 0-8071-1018-3 (pbk.)

Contents

Here is the road . . .

The Inheritance   3

The Onion   6

Invisible Work   7

Ice Storm   8

Harvest   9

After Surgery   10

Subtle Wisdom   11

Small Rain   12

Narcissism   13

Learning a New Language   15

Crafts   16

Affirmations   17

Long Walks in the Afternoon   19

the far reach . . .

Wars   23

Stasis   25

Journey   26

Fasting 6 Days   27

Burning the Root   30

Blue Zone   31

Dear Joanne, This Morning   32

To Speak of Chile   33

Fugitive   34

Unwritten History   38

Radiation   40

**the long sweep of wind
toward morning. . . .**

October Elegy   45

Country Woman Elegy   47

Catechism Elegy   48

Elegy for a Sister   50

Unborn Child Elegy   52

Glass Elegy   54

April Elegy   56

Gemini Elegy   58

Onion Elegy   59

Fire Elegy   61

Notes to the Poems   63

There is a dim glimmering of light unput out in men.
Let them walk, let them walk, that the darkness overtake
them not.

Saint Augustine

You do not even have to leave your room. Remain sitting
at your table and listen. Do not even listen, simply wait.
Do not even wait, be still and solitary. The world will
freely offer itself to you to be unmasked, it has no choice,
it will roll in ecstasy at your feet.

Franz Kafka

Here is the road . . .

The Inheritance

At night the pattern of shadow and light above my bed
reminds me of a banister, stairs and a railing.
I hear footsteps coming up. She is holding a candle.
Either it will be my grandmother with her long white
bolt of hair brushed out silk to her knees, or it is
a young girl in a cotton nightgown quietly cupping
a day-old rabbit, dead. And once more I'm there

in the house where the stairs spiral up from the hall,
the wallpaper white like cream still warm from
the cow—the house that burned, the old
country place in my mother's family.
One afternoon when the light was amber I hunted
foundations and woodsearth there and found
one china cup, white, intact.

I heard women in long white dresses, with puffed
sleeves, reading aloud from books with blank pages.
Quietly their voices crossed over each other
like braids, telling the arts of dust and milk, larder
and closet. The fire begins at the hems of their skirts,
so long they brush over the stairs, the floor, even
the chicken yard but never get soiled—

the fire starts at those clean, clean edges and scorches,
a bad iron burning as slow as their voices, pausing
only at intervals when my grandmother pauses,
staring off into space where she sees lined up into sentences
her grandchildren, her future, mute cups she must fill
with milk, with advice. No one notices the fire
crept now to their knees, to the hems of their starched white aprons.

A coal kissed my mouth—the family Bible had
a cover brimstone black. I've carried its burning
cinder beneath my tongue, long obligations of love

listed in a slanted-back, presbyterian print.
Worn at the spine, it descended
through the men in the family. I'll never own it.
Someone else's hands will mend the torn pages
with tape, other hands will tremble in lamplight,
holding a glass to magnify the words, lifting
unsteadily dried flowers a child

saved there decades back. I'll never be able
to tear out the pages, scooping them up by the hands
full, never be able to make from its sturdy black
frame a box for geraniums, cream white
the blooms, manna white.

I'll never thump it as my great grandfather did,
saying, "This is my house, and the Lord's," so loud
the dog slunk out of the room. Oh, everything was
simple then, my mother said, polishing the apples
father never refused, holding a shining one up.

I saw how roundly the light curled around
it, gold. There was no dark side, no disobedience,
no willfulness, lust or adultery, no questions,
no pitfalls, no ambition, no greater knowledge,
no greater love.

⁂

I slept in the house that burned, one hot summer night,
an infant. A blessing to have us together under one roof,
surely grandmother said that as her grown children
made their ways back to their bedrooms, the beds
now strange to their bodies and July hot as fire.
Perhaps there was honeysuckle

and a stir of wind in the curtains, then a billow of white
starch, and lavender scent, and the sheets bloomed
down. I slept in a cloud. Afterwards, they said
there was no one to blame, though the family
scattered like ashes, one chimney left standing
and the wind blowing hard.

The men suffered most—a hangdog, hurt look
hollowed out in their faces. The women had children

and husbands to tend, a slow watchful working of gardens
and cupboards and the long book of memory.
The house was a touchstone, a ruby whose luster
lit up our dark corners.

Even now before sleep, the house reassembles its porches
and windows. From ceiling to gable it gathers the light
like the church of a displaced longing. I'm never content
with the facts, somehow responsible, homing
when even the birds have fled, and night
closes over, a lid of black smoke
and the moon an ember.

The Onion

Mornings when sky is white as dried gristle
and the air's unhealthy, coast
smothered, and you gone
                    I could stay in bed
and be the woman who aches for no reason, each day
a small death of love, cold rage for dinner,
coffee and continental indifference
at dawn.
               Or dream lazily a market day—
bins of fruit and celery, poultry strung up,
loops of garlic and peppers. I'd select one
yellow onion, fist-sized, test its sleek
hardness, haggle and settle a fair price.

Yesterday, a long day measured by shovel
and mattock, a wrestle with roots—
calm and dizzy when I bent over to loosen my shoes
at the finish—I thought
                  if there were splendors,
what few there were, knowledge of them
in me like fire in flint,
I would have them . . .
                 and now I'd say the onion,
I'd have that, too. The work it took,
the soup it flavors, the griefs
innocently it summons.

Invisible Work

Passionately joined to all things visible
she liked days
cold enough to see her breath.
Not to watch her hands in simple work
meant she would vanish.
She said even the woman
who put at an angle   here not there
her vase of reeds chose order,
was an artist.

Years after, I'll move a bowl of gourds
and think of her, wipe a sill of dust,
by canceling it make my mark . . .
place on the glass table
a glass bowl of leaves
almost leaving them in air.
A steep glide
begins.

Each poem I try to set right what last winter
tracking prints through snow I found:
a clean fled space
abruptly there
tracks vanished
as if complicity of hawk or wind had swept
up everything . . .

a miracle
though some would call it common
as a table spread white
with cloth.

Ice Storm

Saplings hoop over.
The pines list, steep and grave.
I want to say *gravid*.

Roofs all over Connecticut give.

Someone somewhere
must be homeless, dark, and drifting
to madness with all this glitter.

Red buds closed into clear ice
seem to swell out.
Plump, I'd say, as currants.

At night the child
I will never give to the universe
for safekeeping

skates over my dreams of the ice crust,
hurtling into all that white.

Harvest

In this room, shelter . . . a sieving of words breathed
quietly, the hum of dizzy wasps . . .
an occasional click of my knife
against the seeds of perfectly grooved, smooth
peaches . . .
        No one has power here
        although this is a place of power . . .
sweet herbs gathered
and hung to dry in the rafters,

elderberry and beet translating themselves to wine . . .
sunlight rising indoors in loaves of barley and wheat.

There is warmth also
in the table waxed and rubbed clean,
a different act of faith illumined.

Why then, in dreams,
does one wing of the house

loom like the afterlife . . . Room after room of elegant
salons, silver forks wrapped in cellophane
and stuck in vases . . .
        chairs like a clan of druids . . .

everything so tight with weight
even the bird with the fluted tail
on the tree out the window
can't budge.

The word *shelter* opens
its tiny hive. One of the wasps flies out of there

and settles, on my hand.

After Surgery

for Ross

A tremor of one cell in a thoughtful head
unfurls vines of thorn
like the spine of a fish.
And it grows there,
not even a whisper of warning.
You wonder what it's rooted in.

That's what I'd said about evil,
about love
and deep imagination's long tap into the dark.
I'd take the vine of grief the surgeon got,
all that he could get,
put it in a bowl of rocks
and store it in a closet—it may bloom,

this branch of the brain a white spray of hyacinth.
This is not a beautiful thought.
Nor rational, or calm.
It is as cold as the Great Void Chang Tsai says
holds opposites in their ring
and flow, all matter
a mere disturbance in the field.

Subtle Wisdom

after Lao Tzu

When you shut the door in my face,

with no bird singing I go to the mountain.
The sky is more still. On a bare branch
I find the knife whose blade is a thread
stretched in the wind. I walk the edge

until it flames to a furnace, a wind
so hot my gold rings whirl and melt.
There's a tree in bloom at the center.
I take a cutting, come back.

Though it's dawn when I open the door,
your silence is winter's—
stone walls pitch with its weight,
stars freeze there.

I show you the flare from the almonds
in the bowl on the table, their pale
small flowers white-hot.

You hold your hands out to them.

We look at each other an hour.

"Now ask me again what I want."

Small Rain

Outside it rains invisibly.
It could be November.
The page I read is a windowpane—
on the other side of the glass the concierge
says her sentences, a French I can't translate.
She watches me through the page,
muttering.
                    Perhaps she tells me her loneliness.
She is tired of the rain, the streets.
Her pots of rosemary no longer please,
her bourgeois lover's left for Spain.

I breathe on the page and imagine a mist,
my finger marking it. I tell her
how she is closer to me than memory,
as close, though I will never touch her,
as my body stiff with bedrest.
We could be lovers.
                    When I try to read my body,
lives simultaneously lived there whisper, pages
of three thousand books stirring in light wind.

Narcissism

When you turn to your dreams, those ancient
brushstrokes on silk, they tell you
give up your eyes.

When you ask for a map, they whisper,
enter your thumbprint. When you say you are lost,
you hear only rain in a ditch on the moon.

Darkness at first is ice. You sheathe yourself
in it. But your mind flexes like hands
before the braille of the keyboard.

You take a deep breath and begin.

When you've learned to see in the dark,
your tongue furls, thick as a shoe.

You can't explain. You can't speak.

You act out *cold* by taking off your clothes,
hunger by circling twice about your bed.

Enough is the cup you would make of your body,
so filled you run over, a lake,
a sea.

When you've learned to speak without words,
the moon's scythe takes off your ears.
Slowly they fall to your feet.
They are shells, quiet

without the wind of your twittering roaring listening
blood inside them. Empty. You wonder
if they ever were yours.

Weren't they more nearly funnels
your mother used to channel her dark longings
into the universe, or the gates your father
slammed shut more than once because he loved
the resonance of echoes?

Not to hear, you'd thought,
would be the color of an unpried pit, walnut black.
But no, its color is the clear green of the horizon
in summer, just after
stormclap.

As you breathe on the mirror, a mist
gathers there, ripens there.
An emptiness seeds know, husks know,
and you in the drifting clouds of your breath
on the mirror
know.

You must give back your dreams.
You must loose them one
by one.

They will fall like slow rain
into wells, ditches, lakes.
When you are ready, you can walk them like bridges,

without reflection know
where to go, what ask, what give.

You will reclaim your own.

Learning a New Language

When I tell you I've waked as if in a basement,
and the windows are open, I can smell roots—
don't do anything, you say, *just stand there.*

And simply, I am waiting.
Even learning Spanish in the evenings
I'm waiting, as if for a stump cut down
years back to send up one sapling
wet with new leaves.

Or sometimes, looking around the room I find you
here on the sofa, head tipped back to music,
learning what it means to open.
Then each new word gives me
your upturned face:
la cara, the face; *la ceja*
eyebrow; *la nariz*, the nose;
temple, *la sien*; *la boca*
the mouth.

And I remember the darkness, how the sea climbs
out of it, and the firmament, and light—
tentative at first, a dawn full of wind
and words that let be.

Crafts

Out here light seams along the ridge poles of old barns
the way a diamond scores glass.
As if the pond's a book of hours

the least shadow
and crease of a duck's wing
is given.

In such light, I begin to see

handmade stitches that take forever in the linens
and quilts folded like pressed
lilies in attic chests—

and dowel marks,
wood that's been feathered or dovetailed—
each stroke

so exact a flash of light
a bird's released from the grain of swamp cedar.

In such light, hands settle to their tasks.
I can see the whittler's blue wrist vein
throb.

I'd be a pulse like that.

Affirmations

see without looking, hear without
listening, breathe without asking
W.H.Auden

1.

An Eskimo shaman
will take stone, and with a pebble sit quietly
for days tracing on stone a circle,
until snow and mind are one.

Gazing into the whirl of a knothole
I sit out winter. Someone mutters inside.
Just one tremor before the walls give me
another white word for snow
this wood desk shimmers, as if wind
had reached wood's spellbound
galaxies and seen
the pole star
turning.

2.

Storm coming, this sky
brews, swelters—a guttural verb.

I listen to Mahler in the darkened living room,
his tumult like birch trees, hundreds
in a limber thrashing against
black sky, light broken
from a source so electric
even the roots shake.
And in all this hear nothing
until the contralto
rises out of the swirl,
vulnerable—

and such a stillness after,
I hear water
begin to bead on the yellow sycamore outside.

3.
The word *death*
lives deep in the oddly branched vines of the lungs.
It is a wind instrument with no stops, a low
whine you ignore because conversation, or the owl's eye
yellow of the sky at dusk, or the solid crack of wood
split for the fire distract and claim you.

I am learning to breathe
without asking for breath to carry me anywhere
but here, to the split second rush before wind
strikes word, to the moment I am what I am
without knowing it.

Long Walks in the Afternoon

Last night the first light frost, and now sycamore
and sumac edge yellow and red in low sun
and indian afternoons. One after another

roads thicken with leaves and the wind
sweeps them fresh as the start of a year.
A friend writes she is tired of being one

on whom nothing is lost, but what choice
is there, how can she close her eyes?
I walk for hours—either

with hands behind my back like a prisoner,
neck craning up to the sky where chain gang
birds in tight nets

fly south—or with hands swinging free at my sides
to the brook, the water so cold it stings
going down. Either way, I whisper

to dogwood, fern, stone walls, and the last
mosquito honing in, *we're in this together.*
Here is the road. Honest dirt

and stone. Some afternoon, heading home before dark,
if I walk by mistake, lost in thought, far beyond
the steep trees, the satellites and stars,

up over the rim to a pitfall, past any memory of words—
even then I can give my body its lead,
still find my way back.

the far reach . . .

Wars

1. Documentary

Men in stout uniforms, helmets like tortoise
shells, glide on parquet,
brush past a carved mantel, rococo and cool.
Empires fall, a voice tells us, slowly.
The rain falls and in it blossoms of smoke
profoundly cease fire.

The narrator, if you believe his voice, tells
history as if it were a thing of the past,
but his voice travels out into waves
of dark galaxies light years away,
the word *war*

grandly pronounced, wonderful as any
Sapphic poem or Persian
shard.

2. An Ordinary Moment Between Wars

It's noon. The whistle blows in air like fetid
fruit. The factories simmer.

As I sit here wondering what to make
of an English veteran I've remembered—
brought to the theatre in a basket,
arms cut off to the collarbone,
legs sheared to the crotch,
compact and speaking of Oscar Wilde,
"All art is useless"—

as I sit here, the workers from Electric Boat
make their run through the company
gates for liquor.

3. Civilians

When my uncle speaks of war,
dignity buttons on him like a linen vest.
Only the Germans were cruel.
When he ridicules Asian peasants,
his feet do a tap dance in their good
leather and brown polished wingtips.

I keep wanting to see them under a chest
of bamboo in Da Nang, in a bedroom
whose walls fly out in one blast
leaving the floor like a tea tray,
one wrought iron railing in place,
the chest, and those terrible
empty shoes.

4. Cold Wars Inside

Asleep
I cross over rivers into a dream, carried by pain
in a gaunt man's face. He reads me ancient
documents. Centuries crack. Old conquerors
leave the left-alive beseeching the moon,
their hands cut off, flung at their feet
like forgotten gloves.

Now morning
snow falls like sand in an hourglass
close-up. History is pain in movement,
Burkhardt said. It was his face in the dream.
My feet touch the cold floor. I move into a day
that opens like any other in history, grand and numb.

Stasis

Watching black water run, glancing up
to the stars in these bold winter skies,
I want only the optical illusion of movement.
I will be pure, as pure as this fringe of ice
forming in the shallows of the brook,
as concentrate as stone. I will stand
here on the stone in the dark and watch
the black water course over rocks and
over the roots of the maple tree
toppled in August, and I will not think.
I will not hear cavalry officer's boots
ring on cobblestones. And not see
you, Rosa Luxembourg, your cold body
slung into a canal long before the war
I was born in. I will say, and for one second
believe, that the self is all we've got left.
I touch wet stone, so cold my skin
nearly sticks. I touch my tongue to the stone.
Clear through to my bones I want to feel
passive as flint, then strike—these fists
filled tight with raw, unthinkable stars.

Journey

Our train speeds north along the coast, careens along its ties
and rails. I spill my coffee on your shirt. I like the taste
of cotton and wet skin. Behind us and our reveries,

by two's our counterparts, waking in fear of their bodies,
smolder. Then the dining cars and towards the rear
dark cribs of coal lie open to bright stars.

Of course one of us should go sailing out the window
like a cosmonaut on a line and float in the updrafts,
in the sparks of the wheels and swoop out over

the water. Are those islands or distant green Chinese
pagodas? The word *timbrel* comes to mind,
the ghost of a face on the glass.

You answer as the train slows, look: a station where
the porter's hands are torn, his skin is cracked,
his belly cold. There's blood in the street,

women in the soup kitchen, empty kids. The rent's
unpaid, the grammar surly. We get off here—
it will be better.

Fasting 6 Days

1.

As an amulet
I wear this bone
locket, a cell door
carved in Chile, the work
of a prisoner. He was tortured, unfed.
Perhaps he never hoped to get out,
or perhaps, more brave, he did—
this door coaxed from the bone of a horse
a testimony, like the ancient stone rolled
out of the mouth of death. With that man
in mind, I fast.

2.

The silence rings
and I salivate on cue, the second day.
A pinch of elation seasons me.
This fasting is a kind of work—
it tries my wind, my hands shake
as they do the first day out
turning the garden's harvest of stone
and dry stalks after winter's
eased up.

The goat sun climbs higher,
an act of pure will.

3.

A fat man comes to mind.
Unable to resist pork pies made
with rancid butter, he gorged. Charity? he said.
Who can care how others will be fed?

In an old text once, I found
a recipe for "distressful bread"—
acorn, fern root, pompion kneaded in.

Records of the poor, you have
to dig for these—

though now my body is the only book
I read.

4.
I would eat anything.

In no dreams now do I recognize myself.
What's a knife for? to carry, just in case.
It's dark in here. I wear skins.
No, I don't want your help.

Whole populations of hungered children,
faint in the light as the moon at dawn,
clamor.

Last night I went through thrift
like a Nazi. I went to the A&P, walked
there quietly past cabbages and onions, past
bins of potatoes.

Among the sullen eggplant I saw
cellophane bundles, young children

dressed hot from the knife.

5.
The many colors of water
quiet me.

Strange to hold my face between my hands,

to think of these days without anger,
and without terror
the long sweep of wind into the night.

6.
At the end of the sixth day, respite.
No feast? you ask, no prodigal
welcome home?

Just what it takes to be steady
makes me tremble,
held here

by the pendulum sway of the trees in rain,
all that weight back and forth,
somehow

like the grief of ancient wordless songs
I'd forgotten until now—

I will dance, you will take me by the waist,
we will sing in the streets.
But first I savor

simply the need to return to the world,
touching slowly the bread you offer
and, carefully, your hand.

Burning the Root

Cedar at first, then a splay of staghorn put to the torch,
it burns, a relic of Georgia O'Keeffe's, in the fireplace.
We distance ourselves from the cedar's simple wood,

shape-changers, making love on the floor.
When smoke curls up one protruding sharp antler
and puffs in the room, you get up, poke the fire,

shift the root. In front of the fire, you turn suddenly,
close-up, a blue movie in my brain. You burn there,
fire licking your horn, your fine fur.

Then we finish and sleep, who knows what secrets
smoking, banked down deep. Though we fit together
simply, like spoons,

the room is a saracen plain, cedar root turned
sacrificial ram on the spit, seen from the underside,
hind legs out stiff.

And it keeps burning, the smoke a curl of contempt
in the wind, not unlike the smoke of a cigarette
held to a bound woman's nipple.

Blue Zone

Since the assault three days ago, the graduate student has not regained
sufficient consciousness to identify her assailant or to recognize her husband.
According to her physician, she is in a partial coma and only screams.

Local newspaper

Into a blue unconscious zone a woman was struck
down days ago, attacked. Alive and not,
still she is screaming, unable to stop
or make time move, unable to call herself back—

all her energy and speech reduced to the one
persistent moment when someone hated
her body, or his own,
enough to do this.

I thought *unconscious* meant a deadly quiet.
I thought pain ripped along the body
tearing the seams, until you mended
and forgot.

Pure terror must have flung her like a stone
far through the dark, into an outer space
where she's weightless, there's no falling back,
unless her scream is her slow descent—

that scream, a color bruise blue
as the grass in a nightmare field struck
open, and used as a slaughter pit for cattle.

Dear Joanne, This Morning

I fall into and out of myself like the mad woman who tries
to write with an unlit candle. When I enter the lives of poor
women—what they eat or if they eat at night, the balance
of light and heat, cold and wet in their clothes, their beds,
in their poems, their gods, their politics—I write,
the summer heat has risen and fled like mist from the pond.
The wind has taken it south of the equator, where it's a hot
wind drying the mildew from torn curtains. An old pickup
down a dirt road scares up the chickens, kills a cat—
but the car runs away like childhood, like the wish for more
light, and I look away from my desk, outside. Whatever I see
is mine. We used a rope, measured rods and links, and marked
our boundaries. I own the land and the pond, borrow the air,
learn what I can from the sun. There's room enough to spread,
enough solitude and wood to burn through a Depression.
Our parents said, be provident. We wanted to go further,
beyond that dust blown from a private past into a private future—
but here we are—a car runs away in the dust, *chickens squawk*
a woman takes the blade of a long knife and tests it against
her thumb—that woman, mirage and not, somehow my old
country aunt, her breath a shimmer of dust in this Mexican
wind swirling up from the page, a summons. All the candles
of ownership blow out. In this rich darkness, family widens—
you are indeed my sister, mad enough and sane to know the far
reach lives can make, beyond their single locations.

To Speak of Chile

Sometimes, what is most real shimmers, a dark
geography of dream—a film off its reel, tangled
on the cutting room floor. Someone edits
what we know.
                    Take Chile, where the songs
of Victor Jara swelled like a harvest—now a film script
of sunflowers spotted with blood, silent banners of smoke.
In the market, a car black as a tornado stops for you,
and you disappear. Chile, a mass grave in a mine,
workers like sacks of potatoes thrown down cellar.

And these are facts. If I am silent, I consent to them.
In such a silence, I could not take my own life into my hands,
rubbing its skin like an apple's. I could not touch it
with the reverence I hold for the newborn, or for the dead
bodies of those I love enough to wash and dress for burial.

Things your hands know, you respect, my exiled friend
Ulises said, up to his elbows in flour, making bread.
And if dignity becomes a habit, as I believe in labor it does,
and in the courage to resist even those who cut off hands—
a man in prison can whisper songs. Ulises Torres did.

Fugitive

Manuel Cortes, socialist mayor of Mijas and a member of the ambulance corps
for the Republicans in the Spanish Civil War, went into hiding in his house after
Franco's victory in 1939. Hidden in a wall for two years, cloistered upstairs
in another house for twenty-eight, he came out of his solitude only when a general
amnesty was declared. Manuel and his wife Juliana and his daughter Maria lived
daily with the fear of discovery, reprisal, and death.

Manuel in the Wall

I am a criminal. They say that. Three landlords
with personal grudges, some privilege,
some power. They sign
a *denuncia*
             and I am a criminal.

When I was a boy, religious old women
sat in their doorways and studied us,
we were fruit in their markets. They buzzed.
They could spot a sinner by the look of his hands,
they said.
             I know my hands.
Nails square, fingers sturdy, scar
on the wrist of the left, the map
of the palm with its long lifeline.
Clean barber's hands
that called meetings to order, cheered
at the *feria*, tied tourniques at Sarrión.
Hands I press between my thighs, here
in the dark wall that fits like a coffin.

Under the black star I was born.
Then smallpox, hands tied to the bedposts,
slow torture. I should have known the signs.
I will lose my life by inches, each breath
an itch—unlike you, *compañero*
Raphael, mayor of Los Boliches. There, across
the slender skins of your wrists you pulled
a bright razor, you bartered the green
horse of your courage for a black
star—a prisoner's exchange,
a choice when there is
no other.

When I was twelve, they brought a man who hadn't paid
his taxes into town half-dead on his mule, hands
tied with a rope. They wanted people to see the flies
stuck to the welts on his back, they wanted us to see
his muscles twitch like a drunkard's eyelids.
He was a small holder. He'd resisted the toughs
who tore the yoke from his ox in the field.
For his courage they took half
his breath and fed the spectacle
to children.

It is perhaps for this I keep alive in the wall's
dark dignity, for this clear memory
I won't go mad—

            although Raphael
still we stumble together in the dark as we did
on the black road to Torrox, over the dead
bodies of our comrades. Sometimes, coming awake
I confuse you, alone in your death,
with myself, alone in the wall. I smell
your breath of onions and feel the cool
dirt of the prison floor against my cheek,
the barber's razor and a relief
of blood.

Then I repeat, like a woman touching an amulet,
"Juliana brings an onion and a bit of bread at twelve,"
and it's not you breathing here, Raphael—

only this man who keeps alive on an onion
and a bit of bread, and is hopeful.
When I close my eyes, threads of daylight
arrange themselves into margins
that could be a door, opening.

Juliana in Hiding

Afternoons, I catch him at the window—
he's pried the oilcloth I nailed there,
an inch or less. The sun is a blade
on his sallow cheek.

He is merely looking out,
he says. Always calm, he has no caution.
We have a common enemy, I tell him—
indiscretion.

I walk about the village
as I choose, with my terrible secret
drawn across my eyes. My face is a wall.
Juliana! they say, how stern and dour!

Inside me a small child stares at the world
as if it were a guardhouse where soldiers
cut the moons from your fingers,
dropping them like dirt to the floor.

Manuel Upstairs

I overhear Juliana tell our daughter,
"Working to make enough to eat—that's what the poor like us
must do, nothing else. Politics? Never."

The door opens, I can hear the street.
Then a turn of the latch, the street shuts like a book.

I sit upstairs with the bundles of dried *esparto*
and braid ropes for baskets, fishing nets, moorings.
The grass is a sound like locusts in the Sierra Moreno.

Time moves back and forth in my fingers
as it has for a history of women, as it does for the many
women of Andalusia who gather, dry, and braid *esparto*—
or hoe and reap fields, or pick olives from the trees on the landlord's
terraces. Their infants in baskets nearby sweat
and itch and cry with illiterate hungers.

Twenty years ago
at midnight, disguised as an old woman, I came
to this house where I've sat upstairs each day
with *esparto* and lullabyes. The grasses
hiss, *old man, what have you become?*

Each night Juliana sleeps through the news
I learn on the shortwave—

Mayor of the radio, she says,

                         can you eat ideas?

Manuel in the Sun

Reporters and teenagers come to this street
and point out my house, open windows and doors.
They say, sit here in the sun. You deserve it.

They want to make of me a public monument.
They look at my face and see a little plaque:
This man suffered for his beliefs.

I quote them speeches, poems against landlords,
the protests we sang at the *feria*. They marvel
at my memory. They adjust their eyes
behind their dark glasses and say,

it's the same, today.

They want an old-style hero, one man oppressed
by circumstance.

A single suffering has no more meaning
than a single nail or hammer has
to the finished table.

Thirty years in hiding—quick to say—
easier than the habits that keep them meek
and alone behind invisible walls.

For them, I grieve.

Unwritten History

If we could shake off our individuality and contemplate the history of the
immediate future with exactly the same detachment and agitation as we
bring to a spectacle of nature—for example, a storm at sea . . .

Jacob Burkhardt

This storm won't be given a woman's name.
It has no calm eye. Nor would you call it
a mirror of human passion.

Although waves of the Atlantic pitch alpine
and green over coastal cities, and cones
of dust dance over the plains

this storm does not uplift. It cannot be
worshiped. It creates no new stars,
no heroes or heroines, no history.

In its full radiance
inks dry in their pens, pencils
flare like matchsticks, film
smokes in the camera.

In the wake of this storm, the wind cuts
as never before, straight through.
We lie down in our bones
like X rays.

Who knows how many years will sift unrecorded
or what fossils will print in the Saharas of salt
where seas used to be.

From some other planet
this storm may be noted as cloudbursts
are now by the crab and the eel—
this apocalypse of ours
jotted down

as a relative movement in the cosmic
dance, an unforeseen quark.

✶

But then
on the horizon of the dream, like a nail
nearly pulled from its plank, there is
one blackened
tree.

In the dark of its inner gestation, years
collect, ring after ring of light,

a memory of men and women walking in parks,
in the mazes of fire thorn, along walls
espaliered with fruit trees. Then

over fields and highways
a litter of satellites, arrowheads, bottles, old gods.
Artifacts that whisper

This is all they could do

This is all they learned

This is all there is

Radiation

a liturgy for August 6 and 9

A Call to Worship

Stand in the sun long enough to remember

that nothing is made without light
spoken so firmly
our flesh is its imprint.

Whirlpool nebula, the eye of the cat, snow
crystals, knotholes, the X-ray diffraction
pattern of beryl—all these echo the original

word that hums in the uncharted mind.
Listen and answer.

Responses

If the corn shrinks into radiant air and our bread
is a burning cinder
                    like chaff we will wither and burn

If the thrush and oriole vanish, borne off in the wind,
unhoused and barren
                    we forget how to sing and to mourn

If our cities and mountains fall into the fields
and sleep with the stones

how can we leaf through old photographs and letters
how summon our lives
                    our hands will be smoke

Confession

The bomb exploded in the air above the city destroyed hospitals markets
houses temples burned thousands in darkened air in radiant air hid them
in rubble one hundred thousand dead. As many lived were crippled diseased

they bled from inside from the mouth from sores in the skin they examined
their children daily for signs scars invisible one day might float to the surface
of the body the next red and poisoned risen from nowhere

We made the scars and the radiant air
We made people invisible as numbers.
We did this.

An Ancient Text

There is a dim glimmering of light
unput out in men. Let them walk, let them walk
that the darkness overtake them not.

Private Meditation

(Shore birds over
the waves dipping and turning their wings together,
their leader invisible, her signal their
common instinct, the long work of years
felt in a moment's flash and veer—

we could be like that.)

Common Prayer

And when we have had enough profit and loss
enough asbestos, coal dust, enough slick
oil and dead fish on the coast; enough
of the chatter and whine and bite
of stale laws and the burn
of invisible ions

then we are ready to notice
light in the gauze of the red dragonfly's wing
and in the spider's web at dusk; ready to walk
through the fallen yellow leaves, renaming
birds and animals.

We will not forget our dead,
We sharpen the scythe until it sings loud
our one original name.

the long sweep of wind
toward morning. . . .

October Elegy

Precisely down invisible threads these oak leaves
fall, leaf by leaf in low afternoon
light. They spindle and settle.
The woods open.

Birds no longer
slide by without my noticing loneliness in the bold
stare of the night sky—a sphere
tight as an onion.
At night I wake to a cry like the tearing of silk.
I listen and listen. There is only an owl.
Again, owl. A dog barks.
A clock persists,
its parody of singlemindedness
heroic.

Then mornings, they begin in mists that lift
towards noon, but first as if you've dreamed them in a deep
breath inward the trees come shyly forward
like ribs. Then the doves,
their breasts the color of hewn
cedar, call and vanish.
No one, you beautiful one just beyond grasp,
slide your fingers along my arms
as gently as you slide down
oak and beech and shagbark
loosening the leaves.

Who's attached to you, *no one* . . . who could be?
In ordinary commotions of grief and joy
you're elusive, a radiance
that flashes so strangely different each time
or so seldom
we say of you, *once in a lifetime*
remembering perhaps a phragmite on fire
in salt-marsh light where river crossed into the Sound

or the blow of light that glanced between mother
and father nakedly, once. Just once
laying the fire, remember how I whistled,
myself entirely and no one?

No one would say this:
you may as well laugh in delight,
cut loose. Interpret in a moment's
surrender your heart.

I watch the oak leaves fall.
Surely by the time I'm old I'll be ready . . .
surely by then I'll have gathered loose moments
and let them go, no longer dreaming on the stair
sun-hazy, surely not the old woman who thinks that by ninety
she'll wake once, if a split-second only,
and live.

No one, if I were able to forget you, or find you, I might learn
to enter the cup I am washing, door I am closing, word
I am opening with careful incision, lover or child
embracing—
                    and fall towards that moment fire cracks
from common stones, a sunrise in evening.

Country Woman Elegy

With a hush in their voices
country people round here tell of the woman who walked
bareheaded in winter, keening aloud,
three days wandering with her seven-month child
dead inside her. She wouldn't be comforted,
she held her loss.

Telling this
the old men shake fear from their eyes as they might
shake rain from a hat or coat. Her madness they blame
on winter, the cold and closed-in weather.

I love that woman's fearless
mourning. The child dead, no help for that,
she had to wait until her wanting to love the child
died out in echo and outcry against bare stone.
She had to walk, nevermind the cold,
until she learned what she needed
to learn, letting go.

And I love those reticent men.
They know how most of us strain to ignore our dead,
the woman less fortunate to feel the weight of hers.
Who wants to admit death's there inside, more privy
to our secrets than any lover, and love
a kind of grief?

Therefore we dream.
Last night a wild, purple bougainvillea bloomed in sleep.
I thought to gather a handful, but the stalks broke
like straws, and the wind
took them

and drove them past that woman
bareheaded on the winter road, that woman whose cries
unwound and wouldn't be comforted by love or a lover's body,
by childhood or any piety.

Catechism Elegy

All night the long rain encloses the house
and I wake in quick confusion, as if the slow
winter wasp I'd seen inside the window last week
had stung my throat. I'm held in a dark hive,
struggling to speak.

As deeply as years, around me you curve your parenthesis,
mother and father. Never far from you, or near,
even in dreams I listen for questions that gather

unnoticed. *Where are you? Where's your sister?*
Who are you? What have you done?

You taught me to love these questions like milk.
Daily I was to sound them, echo, and compel an inner life
so rich I'd pour through a hole in the cosmos,
a white river spilled from a source
still and invisible.

But they aren't the questions curved by your intimate
own pain, not the ones that curled their small
fists and knocked, asking in vain for breath
to unlock them.

These I heard at night when I'd stand
at the door of my room, listening.
I wasn't afraid of the dark,

only the sound of your breathing across the hall—
ragged, as if you struggled with an exacting
angel, a wrestling out of the ground
dark roots, or a sowing of stone.

I held back my longing to wake you.
What would you say?

And now, as the long rain circles
the house I hear—as in sleep I hear dreams blow
against me like gusts of rain—your voices
wake me.

Whether they unfurl from the narrow solitude of death
or from the wider one of love, I cannot tell.
You ask me

What can you give? What have you abandoned?
For whom are you poor enough?

and I want to answer *death* to all three, to let the long
sigh of it smooth and diminish
your discontent.
                    Isn't this what you want?

For the sting of death hummed in our daily bread,
it sweetened the coffee, it hemmed in the moment,
it sharpened the rude intent of our silence.

It was there, like a lemon held invisibly in your hands,
the only answer no one questioned,
a radiance that ripened.

Elegy for a Sister

One thing to sing to lovers
who humanly, with their summer hands
quickened me beyond words and mirrors, beyond still-life
banquets of mangoes and cold milk.
                              Another to sing them forward
now that the ground is locked, ruts frozen, and only
canyons of white wind open. Now if lovers lament their secrets
they wear Eskimo masks, each mouth a rigid zero's
cry of pain so like remembered pleasure
it's hard to know the cries apart.

If I were primitive enough, I'd give blood
to the ground. I'd respect what I've killed.
                              I put on the ancient mask
and see tracks, deer and rabbit, blaze in the moon's light.
Shadows breathe. My breath's white tunnel
streams out, numinous.

I conjure forth silences
which for years inside me like charred wood
randomly smoked.

Silence should burn clean.
But here, alone on this cold ground, without lover
mirror, father, mother
still I am double.
                              You rise in the smoke of my breath,
blood sister. There's a myth I would tell you, a murder.
How I invented you, fattened you on sins
that smeared like butter. I kept myself thin.

We shared a father lost in furious distance,
a mother bent on sundering. I needed you as figure
needs ground, you as a woman who follows behind
with a heavy jug and a whetstone.

I purged dark anger, you hid the blood.
You honed my mind to such clairities!
so discreet, my silent partner,
I haven't known I was haunted.
                              But the moon is clear about that
tonight. She burns clean through my memory's blind spot
until you are more flesh and blood
than I.

If you would breathe with me, sister—alive
to the skin as pleasure, alive as pain—
I think I could climb to the rim of my fear and swing out so far
mountains defy gravity, and stars
float like water lilies, near.

But the wind is cold, the wind is wide.
How shall I fill this emptiness?

You offer the heavy jug, and I drink.
This is sweeter than milk,
how my ghost heart fills.

Unborn Child Elegy

Tell me a story
                         whispers my always unborn child
and I pause, listening. Whenever a word
shapes itself outward in speech
there's a hush.
                    In the beginning, I tell her, nothing—
if you can imagine nothing. Just so, and patiently, the ancient
stories begin.
                    Once, lying down in the backseat of my parents'
car—their heads dark on the windshield, telephone poles
outside and the heads of trees blown back against the stars—
I tried to imagine nothing. Warm air rushed on my eyes
erasing the car, the trees, the stars. I inched across
a bridge of thread called emptiness, cold.

Then I knew you were there inside,
asleep in one of the body's seedbeds.
I could hold my breath and find
you, small as a syllable,
a grain like pearled barley in the hourglass of my brain,
a stitch in my side.

We made a pact. I'd bring the world inside,
the moon your heart,
a dark plum your eyesight.
You'd bring me so close to the unspoken I'd shake,
some of the mystery spilling like salt.

Today snow sparks the air like mica—the sun's
just so, cocked right angles to the wind.
I bring you the snow and it isn't enough.
You whisper you want to be born.

I study your whisper, I study my fear.
You're bound, my mother said, to pain.
Each child pries you open.

No one will believe
how alive and present to me you are if I refuse
you a body. But I believe in nothing, a transparent
breath from which all form and color rise
in a passion of wings and leaves.

In the ancient stories, the world begins by surprise
when zero speaks, from mere words
weaving sun and moon, the fire
the flash of snow.

Be the zero who speaks for me.
Be birth and death, the emptiness
only a child, and never a child, can fill.

Glass Elegy

The day she went mad, she watched white sun
emerge from the oaks, shaking loose
the dark as you'd knock garden dirt from an onion.
At breakfast, though we're just now putting in seed,
her talk ran to harvest.
                              Out here, she said, I'm transparent,
a single bloom in a glass bowl of water. I don't need
mirrors, I don't need field.

Later she came back to the house, scattered.
Her hands had flown from her like birds in high wind,
vanishing in a rent of air between trees.

During the worst she lost her eyes,
her ears, her tongue. The glass bowl cracked. She couldn't
recover her collarbone, her right foot, her left breast.
And because I'd learned to talk to her as I would
to myself alone in a room, I tried
to go with her, eyes shut
into the suck of black wind.

Hold still! she cried.

She'd been so long in front of mirrors,
an image in glass, a glass bloom in a bowl—
                                        and when she broke through,
the woods moved in quick, everything out there
verb, quicksilver changes. And these swallow you
unless you turn mirror yourself, and the world
flashes from you each moment.

And then she was quiet.

I can't account for her words that morning, what she later
saw, or the calm finally out of which she spoke
with such authority.

She described a random, long walk in the afternoon
when the woods breathed with her
and she lived through the power
of death and the earth's
rotation

as ordinarily
you do, she said, if you're ready to notice.

In the mirror that evening, dark branches tangled
weaving my face with their fire, and almost
I could reach through and touch the ripening

long sweep of wind toward morning.

April Elegy

In a hush, as if it's still morning, randomly the doves
call and vanish. The dark oaks stretch,
each one anonymous and lean.

No one, I know who you are.
Men have struggled with you in the dark and cried,
built ladders and steeples in your name
and killed. Women in labor, great
as the moon, have dreamed the original
faces of their children—yours—

the face of all waters,
green fire at the margins of leaves.
Without you the dark is a bowl of bare earth.

An old woman told me
the earth, one year too tired, would shrug and roll over.
"People don't change," she said. "They grow more like themselves."
She couldn't imagine new faces. In crowds, in dreams the same faces
came stale and hard as slices of bread thrown out for jays.

But today the shagbark waked—gracefully, a Shiva
with his many arms. The shagbark flashed,
its tapered buds split sideways
and shook into the wind
green fans.

The trees snatch from the moon
buds like tight fists. They grasp and let go
green fire.

Just now at dusk the oaks are steep and black against a sky
white as silk, new leaves so faintly kindled
they don't reflect in the pond, only
the stark trunks show.

No one, you're there, the fire of the many
leaves we don't see in the pond. The mist is your smoke.
I am your smoke.

In the fire and smoke of each moment, my blood unbraids.
Green birds fill the dark.

Gemini Elegy

You are not here, I cannot touch you, or be still.

I walk out of the house to watch the stars, and stay
hours after the last plume of smoke from the chimney.
Wind in his ribs, the Bear tips his nose to the east,
keen for the dawn.

I walk these ridges on a tilted light. I look for the orchid
whose blossom floats from its slender stalk, the one
the Greeks knew resembled the scrotum, wildflower
delicate between your thighs.

Through hemlocks and oaks I hear an owl cry,
low. Breath only, but it startles—like that first
forlorn gasp of hunger, pretext enough
for a lifetime's headlong desire.
                                        And the stars—
every one of them speeds out of breath towards the rim, apart.
Even Polaris, even the Twins, our Gemini lovers, their hands
joined in a single star, distant
so distant their feet, on fire, walk
calmly into the River of Milk.

Even ordinary lovers suspect
they must rid themselves of desire. But to take
expectation by the taproot and keep tugging on the line
coiling it, that takes inhuman effort.
And to hang the coiled root on a nail in the sunroom like garlic,
not as a trophy but as seasoning for soup, that takes a wisdom
we require only of mothers, old women, saints.

Yesterday I planted wild iris in the morning's low mist and woodsearth
by a shelf of rock near the brook. I felt as though I were tending
your body—it is such gentle work—and the roots,
dark threads, brushed wetly over my hands
like nerves, quickening.

Onion Elegy

Hour after hour,
gathering wild onions from the banks of Main brook,
I follow the old worn way of knowing the world. At first
I see simply onions, then lopsided pearls with green shoots
so forked they resemble the tails of exotic fish. Now
they are once more onions, simply onions.
My hands smell of onions,
so does the wind. By noon I am talking to myself like an ancient
herbalist who's studied, and remembers, the small preparations
old men and women make before they die. At last

they turn loose of old furniture and letters, they turn
mirrors to the walls and stare out windows, dreaming
of pod-shaped boats stocked with picnic lunches,
with books that are dog-eared, new shoes and worn
socks, the buttons lost from a favorite shirt.

Suddenly they have the vision of telescopes.
They focus down long dirt roads and find
the moment they turned this way, or that,
and a certain aroma of spices faded from the wind,

or a part of themselves they called secret
and never shared clung like beggar's lice
to a stranger's coat and walked off,
unknown.
They grow calm, no longer afraid. How can they lose
themselves in death? Already they are scattered. Still,
they long to be gathered and used. They are humble,
singleminded.
Nothing. No one
The words still haunt.

Whenever I've failed to love emptiness enough, I fall
inward. I hold on to myself, dense as an onion,
as compact, as tightly veiled.

But today the passion to lose myself in work and be quietly
with the dying at their sunlit windows
fills me as air fills a room.
For miles I've followed
this brook in the calm the dying feel

when they put their hands
into a shaft of sunlight

raising the dust.

Fire Elegy

In small numbers the birds are back, one by one, new call notes.
Then by two's the tanagers, bright as struck fire, return
from their winter's ark. And others, suddenly visible
flashes against still trees.
                                        Our bodies are like these birds.
On a signal so clear they don't have to think,
trusting to certain mute scatterings of stars
they just get here, and strike a beginning.

These mornings my blood rings loud, and I wake in time to hear
five and six, seven, echo on the clock upstairs—
and the birds, their cadenzas and solos. Then our outcries,
in passion the low vibrato I make when we strike
the bell of our bodies deeply—all this music
flung out of the body's loneliness.

Just now, polishing a window, I drifted beyond the smooth
and slippery loveliness of glass, beyond the soft
cloth and lemon sweet scent of the water,
dreaming our bodies, polishing them clean
as the spring air that skims
these trees, as light

as this whispering fire along a nerve—and knew
the body's lullaby wish to be bounded and fed, joined
to another's long journeying, a continuous keeping
in touch. Why else, after long migrations, nights
in the ice floes and winds offshore in the Sound,

after heights in the tropics when sun seems nearer
than those oddly shaped pods, the islands below—
why else, after breaking the spell of boundaries,
do we return to each other, lulled
by the rise and fall of our bodies
coming together, on fire.

Thanks to the body
I learn my own call notes. I sing to the horizon,
whose way is to move continually beyond our touching it,
stopping, or seeming to, only at odd
intersections—only last afternoon

I walked down the fireroad that winds through these woods
to a clearing of trees and a field, just as the sun swung
its pendulum down the horizon. This season only,
at this one moment each day, the red
medallion's struck

on the crown of the road, so that every stone flares, and the fireroad,
true to its name, burns each branch and new nest, each thistle and weed,
each crevice the frost made wide in the road—
and the sticks of my body, arms and feet, all
the bones kindle, and I burn with last light

unafraid, part of it.

Notes to the Poems

1. In "Wars," Electric Boat is the Division of General Dynamics, Inc., which makes the Poseidon and Trident submarines.

2. For information about Manuel Cortes and his family I am indebted to Ronald Fraser's book, *In Hiding: The Life of Manuel Cortes* (New York, 1972). Fraser interviewed the Cortes family and recorded their words. In the poem, I have occasionally taken directly or paraphrased some of the words of Manuel and Juliana Cortes as reported by Fraser.

3. In "Unwritten History," the word *quark* is used somewhat metaphorically. In physics, quarks are elementary entities whose existence has been postulated, although as yet they have not been directly observed.

4. In "Radiation," the ancient text is from Saint Augustine, *The Confessions*, translated by William Watts (New York, 1926), Book X, Chapter xxiii, p. 137.

DATE DUE
